CW00435599

PICTURING SCOTLAND

EDINBURGH

NESS PUBLISHING

2   Edinburgh Castle at night.

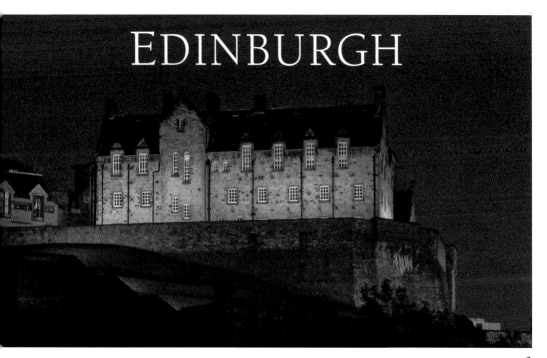

EDINBURGH

Welcome to Edinburgh

Fàilte (welcome) to Edinburgh, the capital of Scotland and one of the most beautiful cities in the world. This is a multi-faceted city, one of hidden depths, elegant vistas, stark contrasts and continual surprises. It is Scotland's centre of government, medicine, law, finance and tourism. Also important are the manufacturing industries of brewing, electronics and publishing. This book will give you a fascinating insight into what is a truly capital city.

Edinburgh's Origins

'Edinburgh was in 1845 a picturesque, odorous, inconvenient, old fashioned town of about 70,000 inhabitants' (Chambers). However, the story begins much earlier with the Castle Rock first fortified during Roman times, taking the name 'Dunedin' meaning 'Hill Fort'. In 1436 the city became capital of Scotland and continued to thrive until the Union with England in 1707 when its importance diminished as the aristocracy moved south. However, the 18th century also heralded a revival in fortunes with the 'Edinburgh Enlightenment' – an era of building and flourishing of the arts and sciences. Today the city continues to expand and prosper and to discard its sobriquet of 'Auld Reekie'. The aerial picture opposite serves as a map of the centre of Edinburgh. It shows how the character of the New Town on the left differs from the Old Town on the right, the two halves separated by Princes Street Gardens. The enclosing high points of the castle (right), Arthur's Seat (top right) and Calton Hill (upper left) can all be clearly seen.

This picture shows George Street's central position in the New Town (left), running from the green of Charlotte Square straight up to St Andrew Square.

The Castle

Towering 133m/437ft above Edinburgh, perched on a crag of volcanic basalt, the Castle dominates the skyline with breathtaking views over the city and the Firth of Forth beyond. The Castle itself is a gathering of buildings and fortifications, covering seven acres, dating from the early 12th century. The obvious defensive strengths of the site led to James III establishing it as the seat of the Scottish monarchy in 1460.

Today, the Castle houses 'The Honours of Scotland' (the Scottish Crown Jewels), the Stone of Destiny (the ancient Scottish Coronation throne), St Margaret's Chapel (the oldest building in the city), Mons Meg (a massive six ton cannon built in 1449) – and the 'one o'clock gun' which is fired daily. It is also home to the Scottish National War Memorial.

Edinburgh Castle has many fascinating (and some grisly) stories to tell. In the early 1300s it was occupied by the English, but was liberated by a daring night attack led by Sir Thomas Randolph. This involved 30 hand-picked men scaling the near-vertical north face of the castle crag and taking the garrison by surprise.

In 1440 it was the scene of a dastardly political assassination when Sir William Crichton, Keeper of the Castle, invited the teenage Earl of Douglas and his younger brother to a feast (now known as 'The Black Dinner') and afterwards had them beheaded on a trumped-up charge of treason.

Mary, Queen of Scots gave birth to Prince James at the castle in 1566. He became King James VI of Scotland and James I of England.

'Edina!, Scotia's darling seat,
All hail thy palaces and tow'rs,
Where once beneath a monarch's feet
Sat legislations sov'reign pow'rs'

Robert Burns

Edinburgh Castle seen from Calton Hill.

8 A classic Edinburgh panorama, looking down on the New Town from the castle. The National Gallery of Scotland is on The Mound, above the railway tunnel entrance at the bottom of the picture.

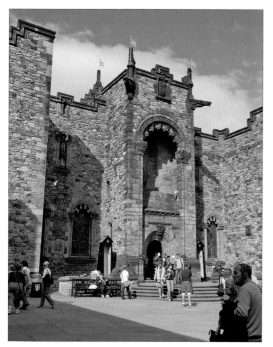 

10 Left: the exterior of the Scottish National War Memorial at Edinburgh Castle.
    Right: Crown Square, Edinburgh Castle.

For many, attending the Royal Edinburgh Military Tattoo is the highlight of a visit to Edinburgh. Set against 11
the world-famous backdrop of Edinburgh Castle, the Tattoo features awe-inspiring colour and variety.

12 St Margaret's Chapel (the oldest part of the castle and the oldest building in Edinburgh), and the St Margaret window, inside the chapel.

From the castle at top left, the Royal Mile bisects the Old Town, running down to Holyrood and the 13 new Scottish Parliament building at bottom right.

The Old Town

'... that in no city in the world so many people live in so little room as in Edinburgh' Daniel Defoe

The 'Royal Mile' is the backbone of Edinburgh's Old Town, with numerous closes and wynds (lanes) branching off it at right angles, giving the appearance of a fish's skeleton from the air.

This is an area steeped in history, housing the largest concentration of historic buildings in Britain, including the medieval townhouse dedicated to John Knox. Lady Stair's House (1622) is now a writers' museum commemorating Robert Burns, Sir Walter Scott and Robert Louis Stevenson. The Tron Kirk (church) is named after the public weighing beam which used to stand outside.

The original Old Town extended from the Castle to the protective city walls at the Netherbow Port. Residents seldom ventured beyond these walls, with the last close in the Netherbow aptly named 'World's End'.

Due to limited space, the 'lands' (high tenements) grew upwards rather than outwards, to as many as 16 storeys and led to Edinburgh being the original city of skyscrapers. Within these 'lands' all classes of society rubbed shoulders, from the aristocracy to the working classes. The well-to-do occupied the lower floors while the poor huddled in the exposed upper storeys.

The 'Mile' thronged with stalls and 'luckenbooths' (lockable shops) and today many of the closes still bear the name of the trade carried out there – Fishmarket, Fleshmarket, Bakehouse, to name but a few.

The Camera Obscura and World of Illusions, left, has the most powerful public telescope in Britain **15** and provides panoramic views over the city, such as this one looking north over the Firth of Forth.

16 Lawnmarket is part of the Royal Mile. Numerous wynds lead off to the many courts of tenements behind, such as this entry to Milnes Court.

Left: Looking down the Royal Mile. Right: Gladstone's Land, a restored merchant's house and 17 booth, built 1617. Situated in the Lawnmarket, it belonged to Thomas Gledstane.

18 The National Library of Scotland is just off the Royal Mile on George IV Bridge. It presents a programme of exhibitions; this is part of the John Murray Archive Exhibition, a permanent display.

St Giles 'Cathedral'

Located on the High Street section of the Royal Mile and on the site of an earlier Celtic church, St Giles is the High Kirk (Parish Church) of Edinburgh and dates from 1120. It was here that John Knox (1513-72) played a key role in the Scottish Reformation of the 1550s–1560s which led to the acceptance of Presbyterianism. St Giles contains many fine stained glass windows, a magnificent organ and the exquisite Thistle Chapel. Officially, it was only a cathedral during two relatively brief periods in the 17th century when the English were trying to impose Episcopalianism on the Scots. However, even today it is still frequently referred to as St Giles Cathedral.

Detail from stained glass window in St Giles. **19**

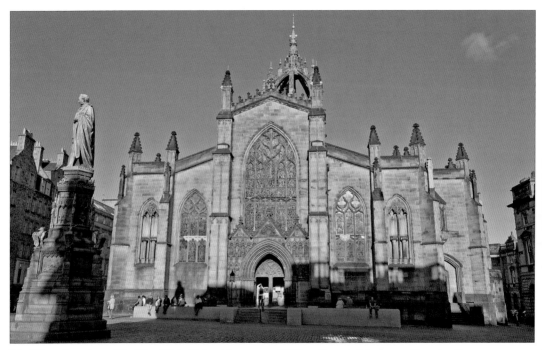

20 West elevation of St Giles High Kirk with statue of Walter Francis Montague Douglas Scott, 2nd Duke of Buccleuch and 7th Duke of Queensferry on the left.

Interior of St Giles High Kirk. **21**

Mary King's Close

The scene on the right may not be a place of beauty, but no visitor to Edinburgh (or resident for that matter) should miss this. Hidden beneath the Royal Mile lies Edinburgh's deepest secret: a warren of hidden 'closes' where real people lived, worked and died. For years they have lain forgotten and abandoned. Mary King's Close is where you can experience the sights, sounds and maybe even smells of an amazing street that time forgot, where everyday people went about their day-to-day lives and where you can now walk in their footsteps. This strange, dark underground site is one of four closes that date back to the 1600s. They were not always underground, but were buried beneath later buildings such as the City Chambers. Astonishingly, the houses that became vaults beneath the new structures continued to be inhabited by those who could not afford anywhere else.

Left: John Knox's house, High Street, just down from St Giles High Kirk. Right: you never know **23** who might entertain you on the Royal Mile, especially during the Edinburgh Festival.

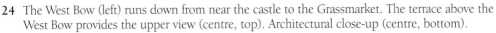

24 The West Bow (left) runs down from near the castle to the Grassmarket. The terrace above the West Bow provides the upper view (centre, top). Architectural close-up (centre, bottom).

The Grassmarket. **25**

26 The view of the Old Town from Princes Street Gardens, with the twin towers of the Church of Scotland Assembly Hall towards the left and Ramsay Gardens on the right.

Some Edinburgh legends

Burke and Hare – 'bodysnatchers' who murdered 16 people to feed the demand for bodies for anatomy demonstrations at the city's medical school.

Deacon Brodie – a town councillor and pillar of the community by day but a daring cat burglar by night and the inspiration for Dr Jekyll and Mr Hyde.

Greyfriars Bobby – a loyal Skye terrier who guarded his master's grave for 14 years and was cared for by local residents, is commemorated in the statue at the top of Candlemaker Row.

Mary King's Close – a busy thoroughfare off the High Street which was sealed off in 1645 to prevent the spread of the plague. Fear and superstition haunts the Close to this day.

The sign outside Deacon Brodie's Tavern and the statue of Greyfriars Bobby. **27**

28 Access to Greyfriars Church is from near Greyfriars Bobby. Opened in 1620, it is famed as the place where the National Covenant was signed in 1638.

This is the George Buchanan window inside Greyfriars Church. In 1570 Buchanan was appointed **29** tutor to the young king James VI and until 1578 also held the office of Lord Privy Seal.

30 The Victorian part of the National Museum of Scotland (formerly the Royal Museum) will re-open in 2011 after a major redevelopment. Two of its more significant exhibits are, left, the Lewis Chessmen of which

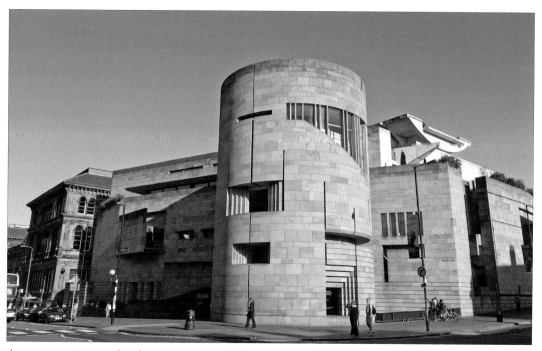

these are two pieces and, right, Bonnie Prince Charlie's travelling canteen. The modern part of the museum, **31** seen above, adjoins the Victorian building and between them they occupy much of Chambers Street.

Edinburgh University

The 'Tounis College' was established in 1583 by the Town Council. The present 'Old Quad' with its imposing dome topped by the statue of the Golden Boy (see opposite), was designed by Robert Adam in 1789 and is considered his most impressive work. The Greek revival interiors are all by William Playfair and his 200ft long upper library is easily one of the grandest neo-classical rooms in Britain. The University itself is internationally famous, particularly in medicine, law and divinity. Edinburgh can boast three other Universities, Heriot-Watt, Napier and Queen Margaret.

Celebrated ex-students include the writers Thomas Carlyle, Robert Louis Stevenson, Sir Walter Scott, Sir Arthur Conan Doyle and Peter Mark Roget. Others include Prof. James Simpson, Charles Darwin, James Hutton and John Witherspoon (signatory of the American Declaration of Independence).

'It is to Edinburgh that we must look for our intellectual tastes'.

Voltaire

McEwan Hall, Bristo Square, is the University of Edinburgh's graduation hall, designed in 1874 by **33** Sir Robert Rowand Anderson. The inside imitates a Greek theatre with two tiers of galleries.

34 Just south of the University, the Meadows provide a recreational space of playing fields and tree-lined avenues, much enjoyed by the student population.

Nearby, Bruntsfield Links are home to one of Edinburgh's oldest golf clubs. **35**
They also provide a fine view of Arthur's Seat.

36 Returning now to the Royal Mile, the lower part of which is called Canongate, where the Tolbooth houses The People's Story. On the left, the Museum of Edinburgh is located in Huntly House.

Left: Canongate Kirk, the building of which was ordained by King James VII in 1688. **37**
Right: Holyrood is at the bottom of Canongate, where stands the Abbey Sanctuary building.

38 This east-Edinburgh view shows the layout of the Holyrood area with Our Dynamic Earth at the bottom, the Scottish Parliament above it and Holyrood Palace to the right.

A closer look at the new Scottish Parliament building, showing the distinctive shapes 39
that have attracted so much attention.

40 Calton Hill from Salisbury Crags with the incomplete National Monument at lower middle and the 30m/100ft-high Calton Tower to its left. The Firth of Forth lies beyond.

Holyroodhouse

At the tail of the Royal Mile, in the imposing shadow of Arthur's Seat, lies the magnificent Baroque Palace of Holyroodhouse; the name 'Holy Rood' or 'Holy Cross' refers to the original Abbey built on the site in 1128. The first Palace was built in 1503 by James IV and added to by successive monarchs. After the 1707 Union and the move to London of the Scottish aristocracy, it became little more than a debtors' sanctuary. However, the fortunes of Holyrood were revived in the 19th century and it remains today the official residence of the Royal family in Scotland.

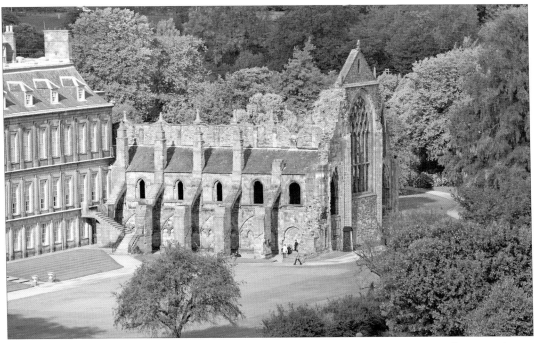

The remains of Holyrood Abbey seen from Salisbury Crags (part of the Arthur's Seat formations). **43**
King David I founded the Abbey, reputedly in gratitude for miraculously surviving a hunting accident.

44 Close to Holyrood, just off Canongate, the historic enclave of White Horse Close dates back to 1623.

'Such dusky grandeur clothed the height,
Where the huge castle holds its state,
And all the steep slope down,
Whose ridgy back heaves to the sky,
Piled deep and massy, close and high,
Mine own romantic town!
                    Attributed to Sir Walter Scott

Another view from Salisbury Crags, a wintry scene looking towards the city centre.

46 On these pages we have an interesting contrast: above is a long-lens view of Edinburgh Castle taken from Salisbury Crags, with Corstorphine Hill to the west of the city in the background …

... while *from* Corstorphine Hill this wintry scene takes in the opposite aspect, with the Castle at 47 upper left and Salisbury Crags just visible through the snow at upper right.

48 At the eastern end of the Arthur's Seat/Salisbury Crags outcrops are the remains of the early 15th-century St Anthony's Chapel. The port of Leith is in the distance.

The peaceful beauty of St Margaret's Loch, below Arthur's Seat, **49** with St Anthony's Chapel on the skyline.

50 Newhailes House, near Musselburgh, is a dignified 17th-century mansion with 18th-century additions. It is in the care of the National Trust for Scotland and open to the public.

Craigmillar Castle is one of the best-preserved castles in Scotland. It was begun in the early **51** 15th century, the earliest part being the L-shaped tower which can be seen in the picture.

52 As we turn our attention to the New Town, we take one last look at the Old Town, specifically the magnificent houses of Ramsay Gardens, as seen from Princes Street in the new city.

Edinburgh's New Town, with Moray Place, Ainslie Place and Randolph Crescent **53** from left to right at the bottom of the picture.

54 Edinburgh's famous Princes Street Gardens. They fill the valley between the Old and New Towns that used to contain the Nor' Loch (see page 64).

Princes Street itself, seen from The Balmoral Hotel. The Scott Monument stands tall on the left, **55** across the street from Jenners, Edinburgh's premier department store.

56 Calton Hill stands at the east end of the New Town and provides an ideal vantage point from which to see the city, especially when sunset silhouettes the skyline. The monument on the right is a

memorial to the Scottish philosopher Dugald Stewart (1753–1828). The Castle is on the left with the tower of The Balmoral Hotel to its right.

58 The lights of The Balmoral Hotel, North Bridge and Waverley station illuminate the Edinburgh night sky.

Floral Clock, Princes Street Gardens – up to 40,000 plants make this the largest clock of its kind **59** in the world. It is also the oldest.

60 The National Gallery of Scotland – located on The Mound, this neo-classical building houses an outstanding collection of works ranging from the renaissance to contemporary artists.

The Mound at night, with the National Gallery of Scotland on the right. **61**
The Bank of Scotland building is on the left.

62 Left: the Walter Scott Monument, Princes Street – climb the 287 steps to the top of this 61m/200ft gothic memorial. Right: statue of the Duke of Wellington situated at Waterloo Place.

The length of Princes Street as seen from Calton Hill. **63**
The three spires of St Mary's Episcopal Cathedral pierce the sky beyond.

The New Town

Plans for Edinburgh's New Town were first proposed in 1752 before James Craig's grid-iron plan of three main streets with squares at either end was finally accepted in 1766. Work on this, the first New Town, was completed in 1791. It was not long before building work began on a second New Town, just to the north, in 1802.

The development of the New Town – the largest area of Georgian urban development in the world – led to 'the great flit' away from the squalor and slums of the Old Town. The Nor' Loch, by this time a polluted and unhealthy lake, was drained to form Princes Street Gardens and the steep causeway of The Mound, connecting Old and New Towns, was completed from the earth dug from the foundations of the New Town. Most of the buildings were constructed using sandstone from the city's Craigleith quarry, once the largest in Scotland.

This golden age of building culminated with the still incomplete National Monument on Calton Hill; supposedly representing the Parthenon, it earned Edinburgh the nickname 'the Athens of the North'. Today the New Town remains an architectural and environmental gem, comprising over 11,000 listed buildings, with many still in residential use. The house pictured is typical of this part of Edinburgh.

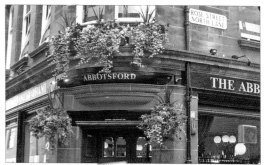

Left: fine architecture in George Street. Right upper: a welcoming watering hole. **65**
Right lower: one of the entrances to Edinburgh's principal department store.

66 St Andrew Square, laid out in 1768, is at the eastern end of George Street. The column in the picture is the Melville Monument, in memory of Henry Dundas, the 1st Viscount Melville.

Since the first edition of this book was published, St Andrew Square has been landscaped and **67** opened up to the public so we can all enjoy this lovely space.

68 Edinburgh is full of characterful bars and restaurants. A particularly fine example is the Café Royal on West Register Street, just off St Andrew Square.

Calton Hill: right of Hamilton's Obelisk is the Dugald Stewart monument, partly hiding **69**
Observatory House. The City Observatory is in the centre. The Governor's House is on the right.

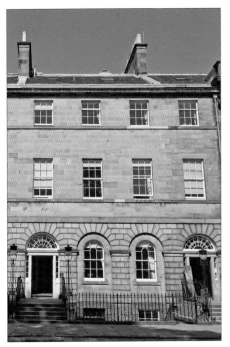

70 The Georgian House – situated in Charlotte Square, this magnificently restored property shows how a prosperous Edinburgh family lived around 1800. Right: the sumptuous Dining Room.

'Lo, stately streets! Lo, squares that court the breeze'

James Craig

Prince Albert's memorial, Charlotte Square. This square is at the opposite end of George Street from St Andrew Square.

72 Salisbury Crags and Arthur's Seat seen from the Pentland Hills. Salisbury Crags' 30m/100ft-high cliff of columnar basalt called 'Samson's Ribs' (left) can be seen to good effect. Arthur's Seat, the 251m/823ft

extinct 'Edinburgh volcano' (right) last erupted over 325million years ago. The surrounding Holyrood
Park, extending to over 650 acres, is one of the grandest open city spaces anywhere in the world.

74 Now to Edinburgh's West End, where an interesting contrast in circular buildings competes for our attention. The Usher Hall on Lothian Road is one of Edinburgh's foremost concert venues …

… while just a few hundred yards away on Morrison Street, the Edinburgh International Conference Centre (EICC) is one of the city's defining buildings of modern times.

76 Looking towards the West End, seen here from the Castle with St Cuthbert's Church (see also p.96) in the foreground and St John's behind it. The Hilton Caledonian Hotel is at top left.

St Mary's Episcopal Cathedral

Situated in the West End of Edinburgh's New Town, St Mary's is the cathedral of the Scottish Episcopal Church and is considered to be the architect Sir George Gilbert Scott's masterpiece. Its existence also owes much to two sisters, Barbara and Mary Walker, who donated the site and much of the money needed for its construction. While it is relatively recent (being consecrated in 1879), it reflects 13th-century style and echoes the ruined abbeys of Kelso and Jedburgh. With three spires and set amid fine lawns, St Mary's creates an image of power and elegance. The Cathedral is unique in Scotland in maintaining daily sung services and is noted for its choir school.

78 Just north of the West End, Dean Village is tucked away in the steep valley of the Water of Leith.

Left: a quiet lane in Dean Village. Right: a tranquil moment on the Water of Leith. **79**

80 High above the village, Dean Bridge carries the main road from Edinburgh to the north.

The Dean Gallery is on the edge of Dean Village and is one of the National Galleries of Scotland.
The scissor-shaped exhibit is George Rickey's *Two Lines Up Excentric VI*.

82 Elegant suburban streets like this one in Stockbridge (just north of the New Town) surround the city.

Another example of suburban style: the geometric precision of a gabled terrace in **83**
Murrayfield Avenue is framed by foliage in this leafy street.

84 Left: even the basements get the floral treatment. Right: a classical statue at St Bernard's Well between Dean Village and Stockbridge.

Lauriston Castle, near Davidson's Mains. Step inside and you will see it just as it was in 1926, **85** when it was left to the nation by the last private owner.

86 Edinburgh is not only famous for Princes Street Gardens. The Royal Botanic Garden, located to the north of the New Town, is renowned for its informal parklands and formal gardens.

The hothouses are home to large numbers of exotic plants.

88 Edinburgh is home to many fine schools, past and present. This used to be Donaldson's School for the Deaf at Haymarket, completed in 1851, which at the time of writing is awaiting redevelopment.

Fettes College, in the suburb of Comely Bank, is one of the best-known **89** independent schools in Scotland.

90 Leith, the ancient port of the city, was Scotland's foremost port and a thriving independent burgh in its own right until it amalgamated with its larger neighbour in 1920.

Leith suffered greatly from the decline in its major industries of shipbuilding and fishing. **91**
More recently however, it has seen a revival of its fortunes.

92 The redevelopment of its dockyards, the opening of many new restaurants and bars, increased cruise liner traffic and the new Scottish Government building (above) have all helped.

The Royal Yacht *Britannia*

Britannia is one of the world's most famous ships. Launched at John Brown's Shipyard in Clydebank in 1953, the Royal Yacht proudly served Queen and country for 44 years. During that time *Britannia* carried The Queen and the Royal Family on 968 official voyages, from the remotest regions of the South Seas to the deepest divides of Antarctica.

In June 1994, the Government announced that Her Majesty's Yacht *Britannia* would be taken out of service. At the beginning of January 1997, *Britannia* set sail from Portsmouth to Hong Kong on her last and longest voyage. On 11 December 1997 *Britannia* was decommissioned at Portsmouth Naval Base in the presence of The Queen, The Duke of Edinburgh and 14 senior members of the Royal Family. Some 2,200 Royal Yacht Officers and Yachtsmen, together with their families, came to witness the ceremony.

The permanent berthing of the Royal Yacht *Britannia* **93** has provided Leith with a major tourist attraction.

94 The pretty village of Cramond lies just north-west of Edinburgh on the shores of the Firth of Forth. Cramond Kirk dates back to the 15th century.

Residents and visitors enjoy a quiet autumn evening on Cramond waterfront. Cramond was **95** originally Caer Amon – the fort on the River Almond, a Roman construction.

'Nisi Dominus Frustra'
('Unless the Lord the city
keeps, the watchmen
watch in vain')
Edinburgh motto

'Coming back to Edinburgh
is to me like coming home'
Charles Dickens

Published 2011 by Ness Publishing, 47 Academy Street, Elgin, Moray, IV30 1LR

Phone 01343 549663 www.nesspublishing.co.uk (First edition published in 2008 entitled *Edinburgh: a pictorial souvenir*)

All photographs © Colin and Eithne Nutt except pp.5, 13 & 53 © Guthrie Aerial Photography; p.11 courtesy of
The Royal Edinburgh Military Tattoo; pp.12 (right), 17 (left), 24/25 centre top, 27 (both), 42, 49, 71 © Callum Whyte;
p.22 courtesy of The Real Mary King's Close; p.30 (both) © National Museums Scotland; pp.45 & 87 © Paul Turner;
p.47 © Duncan MacLaren; p.70 © National Trust for Scotland; p.93 © andy gray digital

Text © Callum Dalziel Cochrane and Colin Nutt
ISBN 978-1-906549-30-5

Front cover: Edinburgh panorama from Calton Hill; p.1: Observatory House, Calton Hill; p.4: statue of Sir Walter Scott
at the Scott Monument; this page: low-relief frieze of the Last Supper in St Cuthbert's Church;
back cover: looking down George Street to West Register House.

For a list of websites and phone numbers please turn over >

Websites and phone numbers (where available) in the order they appear in this book:

Edinburgh Castle: www.historic-scotland.gov.uk (T) 0131 225 9846
Royal Mile: www.edinburgh-royalmile.com
Camera Obscura: www.camera-obscura.co.uk (T) 0131 226 3709
Gladstone's Land: www.nts.org.uk (T) 0844 493 2120
National Library of Scotland: www.nls.uk (T) 0131 623 3700
St Giles' Cathedral: www.stgilescathedral.org.uk (T) 0131 225 9442
Mary King's Close: www.realmarykingsclose.com (T) 08702 430160
The John Knox House: www.scottishstorytellingcentre.co.uk (T) 0131 556 9579
Greyfriars Bobby: www.greyfriarsbobby.co.uk
Greyfriars Church: www.greyfriarskirk.com (T) 0131 225 1900
The National Museum of Scotland: www.nms.ac.uk (T) 0131 225 7534
Edinburgh University: www.ed.ac.uk (T) 0131 650 1000
The People's Story: www.edinburgh.gov.uk (T) 0131 529 4057
Museum of Edinburgh: www.24hourmuseum.org.uk (T) 0131 529 4143
Canongate Kirk: www.canongatekirk.org.uk
Our Dynamic Earth: www.dynamicearth.co.uk (T) 0131 550 7800
The Scottish Parliament Building: www.scottish.parliament.uk (T) 0131 348 5200
The Palace of Holyroodhouse: www.royal.gov.uk (T) 0131 556 5100
Holyrood Park: www.historic-scotland.gov.uk (T) 0131 652 8150
Nelson Monument (Calton Tower): www.edinburgh.gov.uk (T) 0131 556 2716
Newhailes House: www.nts.org.uk (T) 0844 493 2100
Craigmillar Castle: www.historic-scotland.gov.uk (T) 0131 661 4445
The National Gallery of Scotland: www.nationalgalleries.org (T) 0131 624 6200
The Walter Scott Monument: www.edinburgh.gov.uk (T) 0131 529 4068
The Georgian House: www.nts.org.uk (T) 0844 493 2118